EVADING THE ERUPTION

BookLife PUBLISHING

©2023
BookLife Publishing Ltd.
King's Lynn, Norfolk
PE30 4LS, UK

All rights reserved.
Printed in China.

A catalogue record for this book is available from the British Library.

ISBN: 978-1-80505-020-9

Written by:
Charlie Ogden
Adapted by:
Sam Thompson
Edited by:
Kirsty Holmes
Designed by:
Amy Li

All facts, statistics, web addresses and URLs in this book were verified as valid and accurate at time of writing. No responsibility for any changes to external websites or references can be accepted by either the author or publisher.

AN INTRODUCTION TO BOOKLIFE RAPID READERS...

Packed full of gripping topics and twisted tales, BookLife Rapid Readers are perfect for older children looking to propel their reading up to top speed. With three levels based on our planet's fastest animals, children will be able to find the perfect point from which to accelerate their reading journey. From the spooky to the silly, these roaring reads will turn every child at every reading level into a prolific page-turner!

CHEETAH
The fastest animals on land, cheetahs will be taking their first strides as they race to top speed.

MARLIN
The fastest animals under water, marlins will be blasting through their journey.

FALCON
The fastest animals in the air, falcons will be flying at top speed as they tear through the skies.

Photo Credits – Images are courtesy of Shutterstock.com. With thanks to Getty Images, Thinkstock Photo and iStockphoto.
Recurring images – benchart, Anastasiia Veretennikova, Francois Poirier, Slay, PrimeMockup, Panuwach, Net Vector. Cover – Zerbor, jakkapan, Terablete. 4–5 – Roberto Destarac Photo, Deni_Sugandi. 6–7 – 300dpi, EricLiu08, Jagoush. 8–9 – cigdem, Aldona Griskeviciene. 10–11 – Stock-Asso, Simone Migliaro, Frame Stock Footage. 12–13 – Karramba Production, LukaKikina. 14–15 – 4zevar, Alexander Piragis, Ammit Jack, Galyna Andrushko. 16–17 – 4zevar, Markus Mainka, Shark_749. 18–19 – frozenbunn, Kostikova Natalia, Rebellion Works. 20–21 – ahmad zikri, BLUR LIFE 1975. 22–23 – Hadrian, Igor Hotinsky. 24–25 – Anna Violet, Good Luck Photo, Krakenimages.com, TORWAISTUDIO. 26–27 – ja-aljona, Thomas Dekiere. 28–29 – Just dance, Vladimir Konstantinov.

CONTENTS

PAGE 4	Kaboom
PAGE 6	A Volcano… But Super
PAGE 8	Super Science and Supervolcanoes
PAGE 10	Royally Rumbled
PAGE 12	Get to Safety
PAGE 16	Survival Kit
PAGE 20	All Pyro, No Party
PAGE 26	From One Disaster to Another
PAGE 28	A Chilling Change
PAGE 30	Recap: The Disaster Checklist
PAGE 31	Glossary
PAGE 32	Index

Words that look like this are explained in the glossary on page 31.

KABOOM

Do you prefer being warm or cold? How does a room hot enough to melt steel sound?

There is a rumble beneath your feet. You hear a boom in the distance.

IT IS AN ERUPTION...

A <u>volcano</u> has erupted and, well, you are in danger. It is time to become a survival expert.

Keep this book close. You are going to need it.

A VOLCANO...
BUT SUPER

Volcanoes have fascinated us for as long as we can remember. They are very dangerous, yet we build towns and cities beside them.

Imagine a regular volcano. Then, multiply it by 1,000 times in size. Now, you have a supervolcano.

One of the most feared supervolcanoes is in the US. The Yellowstone supervolcano will erupt soon.

'Soon' might mean 25 months, 25 years or 25 <u>centuries</u>. Unfortunately for you, it happened 25 seconds ago. That is why you have picked up this book.

SUPER SCIENCE AND SUPERVOLCANOES

You need to learn about volcanoes. It could help you make your way through the disaster.

The Earth is made up of lots of layers. The outer layer is called the crust. Below the crust is very, very hot melted rock.

The runny rock is called magma. Over time, <u>pressure</u> can build up.

This forces the magma up and out of holes in the crust. These are volcanoes.

Once magma is on land causing chaos, it is called lava. If you see lava… RUN.

ROYALLY RUMBLED

So, you heard the boom. Chances are, you have had some warning, too.

You probably heard the ground rumble beneath you. You might have even felt it shake. You have been in an earthquake!

Once you have felt an earthquake, check the news. Get onto the internet or switch on the TV.

The news will tell you if the earthquake triggered Yellowstone. You already heard the boom. So, you can assume it already has.

GET TO SAFETY

Keep your cool. Ash and rock will soon fall from the sky. Grab your family. Head out of the danger zone.

Pyroclastic zone

The most dangerous area is called the pyroclastic zone. This is the area closest to the supervolcano.

You need to evacuate if you want to survive. North America has been nice, but it is about to be buried under ash.

A few weeks of warning would have allowed you time to get out. You were not so lucky, it seems.

Stop reading. Run for cover, NOW. You must find a good place to hide.

Indoors is your best option. Find a house and get upstairs. The higher you can get, the better.

FIND SHELTER

There might not be any shelter. You will need to get to high ground instead.

No! Do not climb that big mountain with lava running down it! Go up the safe mountain, silly!

15

SURVIVAL KIT

You need to be alert on the way to safety. There might be some supplies you can grab on the way.

Can you find some tinned food from a shop? Grab some. It lasts for a long time.

Can you see any bottled water? Stuff it in a bag and take it with you.

The ash from the eruption will make normal water unsafe. Keep an eye on the news. It will tell you when the water is safe again.

Are you in a house? Good. Rummage through the cupboards. See if you can find a first aid kit.

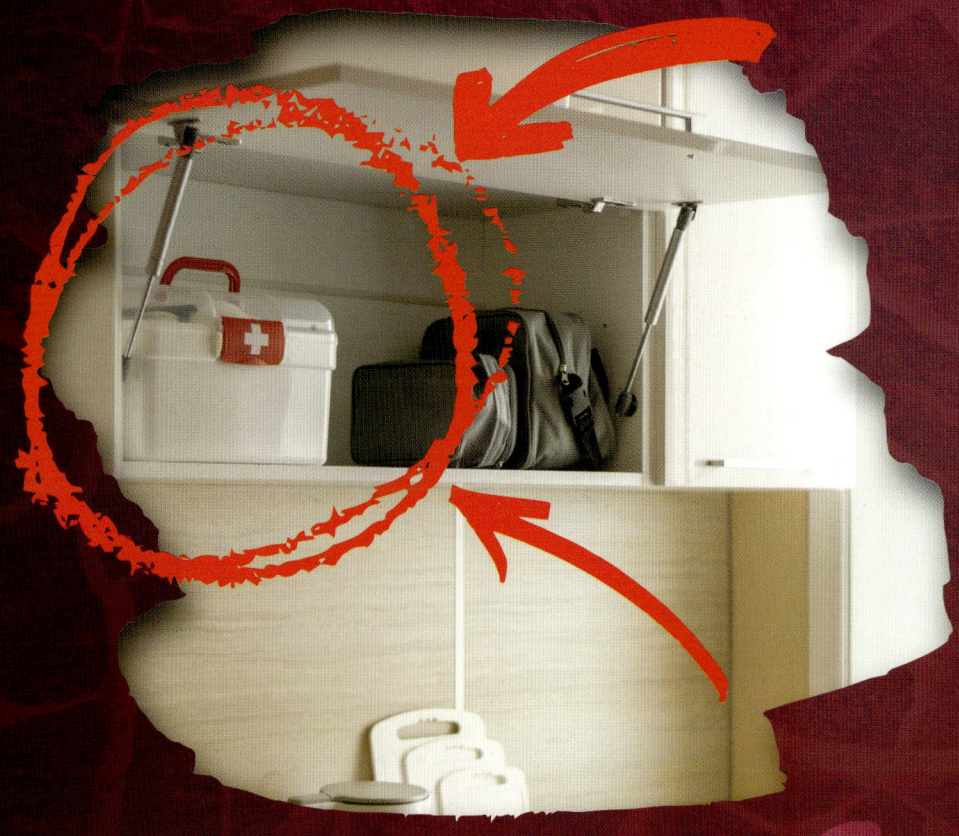

Was that a radio on the mantelpiece? Grab it and turn it to a news station.

The sunlight will be gone soon. The ash will block it out. That means it will be dark both during the day and night.

Do whatever you can to find a torch and batteries. There is not much light or time left.

ALL PYRO, NO PARTY

Pyroclastic flows are made up of fast-moving lava, ash and gases. They might last for a while.

You can spot a pyroclastic flow. It will look like a giant moving cloud. It will flatten forests and farms. Stay well away.

If you are inside, move to the next page. If you are outside, watch out for flying rocks.

- Hide behind walls or rocks.
- Crouch down, facing away from the volcano.
- Protect your head.

These steps could keep you alive.

The ash will make the air unsafe to breathe.

If you are inside, keep all windows and doors closed. Do not open them unless you really have to.

Have you got gaps around your doors? Put damp towels over them to keep ash out.

There will be a day when you need to get more supplies. Make sure your skin is fully covered.

Do not go out unless you have a special mask to stop you breathing in ash.

It is not just ash that will cause problems. There will be volcanic gases in the air, too. Some of them are deadly.

CO_2 is a gas that is usually harmless. We breathe it out! But when there is way too much, it is very harmful.

Other volcanic gases smell bad, like rotten eggs. Gross!

If you can smell it, you are in trouble. Get away from the bad smell or you could die within an hour.

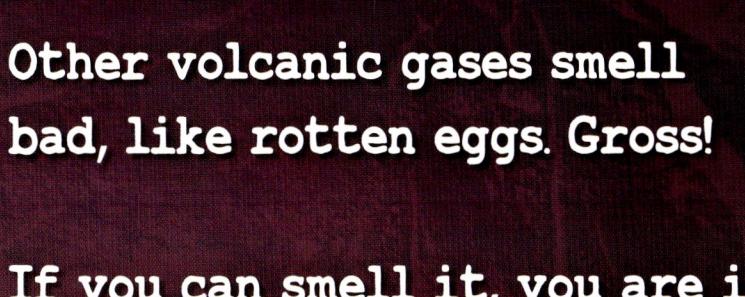

FROM ONE DISASTER TO ANOTHER

Anyone that makes it to page 26 alive is a true survivor. You have lived through a supervolcano blast.

The bad news is that there are probably more disasters on the way. Sorry.

Landslides are when large areas of ground are loose and slip. Cliffs and the sides of mountains can fall. They will crush anything in their path.

Avoid areas such as riverbanks and valleys. Protect your head and stay on the lookout.

A CHILLING CHANGE

Still here on page 28? You are the ultimate survivor. Not many will have made it this far.

The eruption of the Yellowstone supervolcano will change the planet you live on. It is about to get cold.

The clouds from the volcano will block out daylight. Soon, it will be cold and dark everywhere.

Be ready to wait out the big freeze. It could be years before we get back to normal. Good luck... You will need it (and lots of jumpers).

RECAP: THE DISASTER CHECKLIST

How to evade the eruption:

- ☐ Learn about volcanoes.
- ☐ Check the news.
- ☐ Leave the pyroclastic zone.
- ☐ Find shelter or high ground.
- ☐ Find supplies.
- ☐ Close doors and windows.
- ☐ Expect more disasters.

GLOSSARY

CENTURIES   units of one hundred years

CRUST   the hard layer of rock around the outside of the Earth that is split into sections called plates

ERUPTION   an explosion of very hot, melted rock and gases

PRESSURE   a type of continuous force that can push on or against an object

VOLCANO   a mountain that can be formed with hot gases and melted rock

INDEX

ash 12–13, 17, 19–20, 22–24

daylight 29

earthquakes 10–11

food 16

gases 20, 24–25

landslides 27

lava 9, 15, 20

magma 9

news 11, 17–18, 26, 30

pyroclastic flows 20

water 17